A Practical Guide to Opening Your Own Business

By Rupert C. Robertson III

Contents

Introduction

Most people do not want to spend the time required to read a book. Instead, they want instant gratification. This guide is meant to give you the most information and, in the fewest words possible, to aid you in your goal of opening your own business. At the beginning you will find a general outline of what it takes to start a successful business. Further into the guide you will find a checklist plus more specific information on how to get your business up and running. Some of the information is repetitive. There is a reason for that. The points that are repeated are the ones that I consider to be of the utmost importance. There is also guidance on where you can find additional help and more information for your particular product outside of this guide should you need it. No punches are pulled. This information was gathered over the last forty years during which my wife and I have owned a total of ten (actually more) successful businesses. Some of the lessons we learned were brutal. Our hope is that we can save you some of the hard knocks that we experienced. It is your choice to follow or to ignore any of the advice offered here. Yes, we do travel to consult if you feel that you need us. Please contact us for our fee schedule. Our on-site services vary according to your needs and we can do anything from location searches to staff training.

We like to be prepared to work when we get to you and we will do advanced research before we come. This will save you time and money. If you come to us, we have a flat day rate but we might get in some fishing, canoeing or some other more mundane activity during off-hours. We will ask you to come prepared with all the information that you have available to you about your new enterprise so that we can get down to business immediately. We are slave-drivers, as I am sure you will also be, but we will take the time to get to know you so that we can better tailor our information to your needs. There is one important thing to remember. The information that we give to you will only be as good as the information you give to us to base our research on. We can be reached by e-mail at rupert@artelco.com or by mail to Robertson Consulting, 136 Lynn Creek Dr., Fairfield Bay, AR 72088. This is an on-going work and it is refined every time a toe is stubbed or a new lesson is learned.

General Advice

1. Do something! This is the hardest step of all. Everyone has dreams but 99.99% of them are unwilling to get off their couch and do anything about it. You could walk out in the street and shout your best business secret and everyone would go "Wow, I could do that". Then they would get all excited, go home and talk about it for 15 minutes and eventually forget about it as time goes on, having never lifted a finger. Excuses for not getting started are as numerous as the stars in the sky. The only people that succeed are the ones that are willing to put in the

time and effort to do so. You will have to get off your couch and put in the effort. No one is going to give you anything. You have to earn it.

2. Best friends or spouses do not necessarily make the best business partners. I have many friends that I would do anything for but I would not have them involved in my business. On the other hand, my wife is the most dependable person that I have ever worked with and I know that she will always hold up her end of the responsibilities.

3. Be there! Plan on being in your business. No one else will care about your business the way that you do. If you want anything done a certain way, then you will have to be there to assure that it is done that way. Very few small businesses succeed when the owner leaves the shop in the hands of others and spends all of his/her time attending to other projects.

4. Strings. If you are borrowing money for startup, make sure that you know all the strings that are attached. Banks will often want control over the way the money is spent and friends or relatives often want control of your life.

5. Your money. Your Ideas. It is your money that you are spending so spend it the way that you think would be of the most benefit to you. Many people have many ideas that they would love to share with you but you are the one taking all the risks. If they are so smart, why haven't they gone into business on their own and made a million?

6. Get a computer!

7. The Internet. Having access to the internet is a good thing when it comes to both research and acquisition of products. It is the easiest way to find almost anything.

8. Politics and religion do not mix with business unless the business is political or religious in nature.

9. Too good to be true? Get rich quick schemes do work for the person that comes up with them and markets them. They almost never work for the people that buy them. If it were that easy, everyone would be rich.

10. Reality check! Do something that you really want to do and that you think will be fun. If everything goes as planned, you will be dealing with your new business for a long time. It had better be something that you enjoy.

General Business Plan

Before opening your business

1. Keep all of your receipts for any and all expenses.

2. Decide exactly what service or product you want to introduce.

3. Make sure that there is a need or market.

4. Design and develop your product.

5. Cost and pricing. Determine a real cost on your product.

6. Know what you want to market inside and out.

7. Form a marketing plan.

8. Know who can help you develop your business.

9. Check and use free local resources.

10. Learn all you can about the competition.

11. Develop your company's image.

12. Select the location suited to your product.

13. Establish a line of credit and a list of business references.

14. Set up an accounting process.

15. Protect your product and yourself from liability with insurance, incorporation and/or other tools.

16. Advertise

17. Opening your business. Have enough cash up front to cover at least six months total expenses.

18. Hire and train employees.

19. Double check above items and make sure that your idea is still workable and that it is capable of showing a real profit in a reasonable amount of time and that it will allow you to make a reasonable living.

20. Remember, the customer is always right. Offer suggestions to improve what he/she is doing or to save him/her money but in the long run it is their money, so do it their way. Do not argue with the customer about their product. Do not gloat over their mistakes if you warned them it would happen. They can always go elsewhere to do business.

Opening Day

1. Make sure that you have product available.

2. Have all of the tools you need in place.

3. Make sure that everyone that you ever knew or think that you ever will know is aware that you are opening for business.

4. Try and have any and all the media present that is possible for publicity. (Often your local Chamber of Commerce will have a ribbon cutting if you are a member.) Take pictures that can be turned into press releases. Have a Grand Opening, if you can, and hold a drawing or give away prizes. Do anything you can to attract positive, tasteful attention. (Balloons - clowns - lights - an ape - you get the picture)

5. Make everyone feel welcome and that they feel good about being there. Don't just talk to your friends. Make sure you speak to everyone that shows up. Smile. Don't be nervous.

6. Don't worry about sales today. Don't turn down business, but don't force it either.

On-going business

1. Get your accountant/tax consultant to show you ways to save money on taxes and best utilize your business resources.

2. If you are working out of a home, an office, your car or a picnic table in the park, adhere to regular office hours and utilize down time to enhance the business.

3. Advertising always helps. Just make sure that your ads hit your target audience. (For instance, you would not want to advertise your liquor store on a religious radio station.) Always have a good looking sign up at your place of business if zoning allows.

4. Don't get complacent. Continually look for ways to improve every aspect of your business. (Product, marketing, sales, - everything) If the business is standing still, then it will eventually fail.

5. Continue to develop your distribution network, contact lists, client lists and new product lines. Plan to grow.

6. Watch your money. Don't be stingy when it comes to business but do be frugal. Most businesses have up and down periods so plan ahead for the downs by putting something back in the ups. Many businesses fail when the owner tries to live too high a lifestyle for their earning ability or they get used to spending on themselves during an up period and a down period catches up with them.

7. Calculate a budget for both yourself and your business and adhere to it. Spend your money where it will do the most good and always try to get the most bang for the buck. A little money poorly spent is far worse than a lot of money properly invested to produce results.

8. Once your business is opened, you will be asked by many charitable organizations for donations. Pick your donations carefully. Things to keep in mind are which ones do the most good for the community, which ones give you the highest visibility, which ones might accept service instead of monetary donations and which ones might funnel you business later on. (See page # 32)

Working Business Rules

If you are working out of a home, an office, your car or a picnic table in the park, make sure that you adhere to regular office hours. **NEVER OPEN LATE.** (No sleeping in; be showered and properly dressed and in your workplace by starting time and no quitting early no matter how slow it is.) Just because the phone isn't ringing that particular moment doesn't mean it won't in the next. If you must leave the office unattended for any reason make sure you have a phone answering machine that is in good working order and that has a good business message on it. Better yet, have a person in to answer the phone. Many people still have a problem talking to a machine. It is easy to come up with excuses for leaving the work environment. None of them are valid except emergencies. Use dead time to make blind calls on prospects and be sure that with every call you sharpen your phone/people/cold call skills. In case you have never heard of a "cold or blind" call, it means calling a business or individual that you have never met, but might be interested in your service or product. When making cold calls, do not keep people on the phone any longer than it takes to get business done in a pleasant manner. They really don't care about your personal problems, religious beliefs or medical problems. Keep it very polite but short. (Bad habits are easy to form and hard to get rid of. Good work habits are just as easy to form and will stay with you over the years.) Don't get complacent. Continually look for ways to improve every aspect of your business. (Product, marketing, sales, - everything) If the business is standing still, then it will eventually fail. Continue to develop your distribution network, contact lists, client lists and new product lines. Plan to grow.

The Phone

<u>This is very important</u>. Once you start a business that is run out of your house, you can no longer look at your house as a home. It is an office and must be run like one. When the phone is answered it must be in a professional manner. If the kids answer the phone, it still <u>must</u> still be in a professional manner. (Not "My Mom/Dad is out cutting the grass, etc. but rather Ms/Mr. ... is out on a call/in a meeting. May I please take a message and have them get back to you as soon as they return.) Make sure the person's name and phone number is correct. Read the message back to the caller to make sure it is right. You may want to get a friend to call and do a test run with the children so they can practice. Always keep a working pen or pencil and a note-pad by the phone so that an accurate message can be taken. When you check your messages, be sure to call the potential customer(s) back as soon as you can. After business-hours calls can present a problem since you don't normally expect a business call at 9:00 at night. It happens. If you are there, the business is open. The phone must be answered in a professional manner no matter what time it is. All family members must keep this in mind at all times.

Conclusion

This business plan should have given you enough of a foundation to put you well on your way to making your business a success. It's all about inspiring you to take your skills, interests, and talents that you possess and put them to work in a small business or home-based micro-business. It is our deepest hope that your future will be nothing but the best.

More Detailed information

Keep all of your receipts

The moment that you decide that you want to start a business start saving your receipts. Anything that you purchase, rent, spend on upgrades, add to your home, increase service on, etc might be deductible. If you go to the store to buy groceries and pick up a roll of tape to use in the office, circle it on your receipt when you get home and save it. This applies to everything you buy that you use in your business environment. Keep a log in your car to record mileage, even if it's a trip to the post office to buy stamps for your flyers. You will be surprised how quick even small items add up and this habit will help you keep track of your true overall expenses.

Deciding on a product or service

So, you want to open a business. Do you have an idea? What makes you think that this idea has something that people will want to beat down your door to have? Is it so unique that everyone will have to have or use it? Maybe you just think that you can do a better job at a lower price than what is available in your area.

Decide exactly what service or product you want to introduce. It is not enough to say, "I want to open a restaurant". What type of food is to be served? Will it be up-scale, ethnic or home cooking? How many people will you need to seat? Will it be dine in or take-out? Do you need a drive-through window?

These are only a few of the questions that will have to be considered if you are going to open a restaurant, but the same sets of questions can be applied to almost any product or service. What is the bottom line on the nature of the product I want to produce?

Make sure that there is a need or a market

What group(s) of people represent my target audience? Is there a need or market for my product? Is my product or service unique? Why would anyone want what I have to offer?
In other words, who besides me would buy this?

Design and develop your product

Once you have decided on a product or service that you want to market then the work begins. Your main objective should be to have the best of whatever it is you wish to market. Do not be satisfied with the second best. Believe me, your customers won't be. Work out all the bugs and make sure that you have a product that is attractive. Be sure that it will do the job you designed it to do and that there are no hidden consequences such as collateral damage that your product could cause. You would not want to design a child's toy and then discover that there were numerous choking, allergic or fire hazards associated with it. It needs to be packaged in a way that is marketable. Common sense should play a large part in any design.

Cost and Pricing

Determine a real cost on your product. You may have built the first model from scraps or materials that you had laying around the house. That is not representative of the real cost. Take into consideration cost of materials, shipping, assembly, tools, rent, utilities, cost of employees (There are many hidden costs in employing a person. Look into sub-contracting.), marketing, sales, and your own time. Price your product to be competitive and still enable yourself to eat. Price to expand. You may be able to produce your product for one price when you do all the work, but what happens to your costs when you have to bring in help and pay them?

Know what you want to market

Know your product, including where to buy raw materials, packaging materials, etc. Find everything you can about all aspects of your product. (Know the manufacturers. Call them and ask specifically for several distributors that carry the product(s) that you want to buy. Call the competitors and ask if they manufacture a similar product and who their distributors are. That way you are equipped to comparison shop for best pricing so you can maximize profits. Work at developing a network of resources.)

Marketing Plans

Marketing covers everything from packaging to distribution. Random House describes marketing as "Activities involved in moving goods and services from producer to consumer: market research, advertising, promotion, distribution, and sales". Thus, marketing becomes the heart and soul of your new business.

Form a marketing plan. You will have a budget that you will have to work from. It will be up to you on how your marketing dollars are spent. You will need to formulate a plan that will allow you to reach as many people, in your target audience, that you can at the lowest <u>effective</u> cost.

Your product or service needs to be packaged in a way that is marketable. How do you package a service? With words! You simply describe your service in a way that will compel others to seek you out and utilize what you are offering. If you have a physical product, you will have to design the packaging so that people will want to pick it up and take it home with them. A simple rule to keep in mind is to design the packaging for your target <u>buyer</u>. A dog will never buy a can of dog food so the packaging must be aimed at the dog's owner. A kid will whine and nag about a toy until the parents give in and buy it for him/her. Who is your target here?

Know who can help you develop your business.

Compile a list of business prospects and contacts. (This can be from past sales, friends or just people that you know. Don't discount anyone. No matter who they are, they know other people.)

Check and use free local resources

Check and use free local resources such as your local colleges, SCORE, small business development centers, the vast array of state and federal government agencies and other economic development agencies to see what help is available to you. The most important single aspect of getting help is to ask for it. There are only two answers in life; yes and no. If you never ask, then the answer is always no. Even if the particular agency that you have contacted is not in a position to aid your cause, they can often refer you to other organizations that will be in a position to help or advise you. Their advice is good and they can often help you make valuable contacts. Show some initiative and don't expect anything to be handed to you. This gains respect. The internet can also provide you with some help in researching what is out there in the way of help.

The 10 Best Resources

1. Score is an organization of over 11,000 retired and working business executives that offers free business counseling and advise. Check out their web-site at www.score.org for some great ways to help your business succeed.

2. The U. S. Small Business Administration (SBA) is a government agency that is a good source of free information and loans. Contact them and ask for your SBA Startup Kit. http://www.sba.gov/starting/indexstartup.html

3. Your local Chamber of Commerce can be a great source of information and help if they are an active Chamber and not too mired down in local politics. You should join your Chamber of Commerce and be active in it. If you don't like the way it is run then work to make it better. In most communities they do a lot of good.

4. Your local college or university's school of business usually provides free or low cost help in business development and many other areas. The information that they provide can be very valuable. They can also be a source of student workers for part time help.

5. State and city sponsored business development centers are another source of good information. They have seminars and classes, can provide contacts and help you develop plans plus they offer many other services. The development centers that I have dealt with have bent over backward to try and help in any way they can.

6. Industrial and Economic development groups, in you area, can inform you of the incentives that are being offered in that area in order to get your business to locate there. Check with them.

7. Small Business Search Engines... Articles, Small Business Startup Information, Guides, Net Links, Business Centers, Startups, Government, Associations, Assistance http://www.businessnation.com/library/articles/pages/

8. Other business people. I would not interview the direct competition in the area that I have chosen for my business. Look

at surrounding towns or counties and find a similar size or type of business to the one you are planning and schedule appointments to sit down and talk to them (if they are willing). Explain up front that you want to start a business and want to pick their brain on the subject. Do not waste their time. Have a prepared list of questions when you walk into the meeting. Remember, these people are aware of the ins and outs of the local community and can provide valuable insight toward succeeding. Interview more than one, take notes and compare the information with what you have already learned. Some businesses, like Bed and Breakfast's, have conventions meant to help people work together, improve their products and share problem solving. Look on the internet for such groups.

9. Yahoo Small business information. They have articles and can give you a loads of good ideas to work from or incorporate into your own plan. Check them out. http://www.yahoo.com/Business/Small_Business_Information/

10. The Internet. On the internet there are over 59,000 web sites that offer business startup assistance and information. Just type in "business startup assistance" in the search window of your home page and you will be amazed at what shows up.

Know the competition

Is there competition? You had better believe it. If it is not openly apparent in the near vicinity to where you are placing your business, then it is just across town, being offered out the back of someone's home or it is on the internet. Unless you are the rare exception that has a totally unique product or service, there is always competition. Do not be afraid to walk into the business of a competitor and look at the way they are displaying and marketing their product. Look at a price list. Is the sales staff helpful? Are they smiling or complaining? Are they knowledgeable about the product and competent to handle questions or are they just there for the money? Is the business neat? Do you have friends that shop there? What do they like about the business? What do they dislike?

Company Image

Develop a company logo and motto. (This sounds silly but it looks good on cards, letterheads and invoices and people do pay attention to it.) Establish or re-affirm Company Name (incorporate or register the business' name. Obtain necessary permits, etc.) If you plan to grow, make certain that your business name does not limit that growth. For example: Starting your company under the name of "Acme Fence Company" and then trying to branch into landscaping or general contracting. Your company logo is also important. People may not remember your name but they might remember a good graphic image.

Join the Chamber of Commerce, The Better Business Bureau and check into professional
organizations. Display certificates and awards on the walls of your business. This adds respectability to your name and helps make people want to do business with you. Tasteful art on display helps develop your business setting. If the art has something to do with your business, all the better.

Location

Select the work place/space where you will conduct business and see that it is properly prepared for the business that you want to conduct. If you are going to have a retail business, be sure that your store is in a location that will give the public access to your product. Does it have good visibility from the street? Is there so much traffic that it will be difficult for people to get in and out of your parking lot? Is there enough parking space? Think of the businesses that you frequent: what makes them convenient and accessible? Apply those criteria to your site. Specialty stores are not as vulnerable to location, since the public will search them out if it is a product that they need and can't find anywhere else. Be sure that the location is suited to your product. Cheap rent in a bad location accomplishes nothing. City zoning regulations can play a large part in selecting a location. For instance, in some states, businesses that sell alcoholic beverages can not be within 300 feet of a church or school.

If your business is run out of your home, have a dedicated workspace or office. It needs to be "walled in" or separated by barriers to be considered dedicated. There are several reasons why this is important. First, it separates you from the lawn that needs to be mowed, the dirty dishes, laundry and other mundane chores. It insulates you from non-business influences. But perhaps the most important reason is financial. You are allowed to deduct dedicated business space off your taxes in most states. You also need to check with your accountant about deducting percentages from your utilities, insurance, repairs, etc.

Credit and References

Establish line of credit. (Obtain equity loan or have monies available for use. They can be your own funds, but have them in a bank that will write you a letter of credit.) Have a list of business references and credit references prepared when you approach the bank. Every time you complete a service, ask for a letter of reference from your client. If your business involves making physical changes or improvements to items or property, take before and after pictures. This is good for your portfolio and it flatters the customer and makes them feel important.

Accounting

Get an accountant. Search for an accountant that will best serve your needs and will be able to give you sound financial advice. A good accountant will save you more on your taxes than they will cost, plus you get the added benefit of having a financial consultant. Work with your accountant to set up an accounting process that will allow you to keep an accurate track on your costs and, in the future, your profits. Be accurate with your figures so that neither of you gets into trouble with the IRS. An accountant may not always be necessary at first, but it should be assumed that you would grow to the point of needing one.

Protection

Protect your product through copyrights/patents/laws from being ripped off. Protect your name and/or the name of your company, if it is different. Protect your product and yourself from liability with insurance, incorporation and/or other tools.

About Insurance

Insurance coverage should be as automatic as blinking your eyes in a snowstorm.

About personal insurance: You should have enough life insurance to pay off all loans, bills, invoices, cover funeral expenses and give your mate a little room to make decisions in case of your untimely demise. Many people buy whole life insurance.

I personally like the idea of pricing whole life insurance and then buying term insurance and investing the difference. This provides you with the same amount of coverage should you die and gives you the added benefit of a retirement fund.

Look for an agent that carries all types of insurance. When it comes to business insurance there are many agents who specialize in this type of coverage. Ask other business owners, preferably those in a similar business or ones who have been in business for a number of years, what their experiences have been with different companies. Someone who has actually had a claim can really open your eyes.

About property insurance: You should always carry enough insurance to completely cover rebuilding and restocking. If you are leasing space, you will probably be required to carry a specified amount to cover anything that happens to the building and surrounding areas.

About liability insurance: A couple of simple rules are 1.) the more contact with the public, the more insurance needed, 2.) and the larger the possibility of damage to persons or property by your product, the more insurance needed. If you are leasing space you may be required to carry a specified amount of liability insurance to protect the owner of the building as well.

Other types of insurance: There are many other forms that insurance can take that are related to specific products, processes or distribution methods. Chances are, if you are worried about any given area of your business, then you probably need insurance against that worry.

Advertising

Advertising always helps. You should begin by pre-advertising the date that you are going to open. If you are going into the retail side, make sure that you allow plenty of time on the opening date to renovate and to get your equipment and product in place. Make sure that your ads hit your target audience. (For instance, you would not want to advertise your liquor store on a religious radio station.) Always have a good looking sign up at your place of business if zoning allows.

Ways to advertise:

1. Your best advertising will be word of mouth. If you have satisfied customers then they will sing your praises. Of course, if you have a bad product, are rude, late to open, don't seem to know what you are doing and so forth, they will talk about that as well. Very important. Compile a list of business prospects and contacts. (This can be from past sales, friends or just people that you know. Don't discount anyone. No matter who they are, they know other people.) Cater to these people up front to help get the ball rolling.

2. Signs. They can't find you if they don't know you are there. An attractive sign will cost some money, but that can't be helped. Put a sign at the head of your list and make sure that you get one that gives the message that you want to get across. It is a once every 3 years, or so, cash outlay but it is a necessity. Be sure it is well lighted and can be seen in both directions. Check with your town to make sure that there are no ordinances against what you have in mind. Then go for it. So what if the sign is bigger than the store. People will stop in if they know you are there.

3. A free way to advertise is to have a media event. When your have your grand opening, make sure that you notify your local

paper(s), TV station(s), business paper(s) and trade publications. The same thing goes for: an open house, a customer party, you add a new line, expand your business or service, hire a new person, get an award, get nominated for an award, present an award, receive community or professional recognition, change locations or any other positive event. If you are going to issue press releases, it helps if you have a good picture to go with it for the print media. Don't be disappointed if everyone doesn't show up. Quite often the press has too much on their plate to cover everything. If you have a good press release with a picture they may run it without showing up, particularly with smaller papers. Do not forget your address or phone number. I can't tell you how many times I've seen an ad or a write-up and don't have a clue as to where the business is located. Don't make a potential customer work too hard to find you.

4. Join your local chamber of commerce and Better Business Bureau. Most of them have web-sites that you can post your business on for free. They usually provide free links to your home page as well. The Chamber will usually show up for grand openings, ribbon cuttings, etc. and can aid in making it a media event.

5. The cheapest way to reach people is classified advertising in newspapers. Check and see if your state has a press service. (Over 40 of them do.) One state will put your 25 word classified ad in 117 papers state-wide for a cost of $199.00. Small local newspapers will usually run a classified ad for under $5.00. It is important to keep at least a small classified ad in front of the public all the time.

6. Flyers. You can target a specific area of homes and put flyers in their doors fairly inexpensive. It is time consuming but you can always hire neighborhood kids to put them out for you. If you go this route you will need to go behind the kids to see if they were actually placed on doors and to be sure that they did not toss

them in a ditch somewhere. Do not put them in mailboxes. (It's illegal.) How do you know if the flyers are working? Put a coupon on the flyer and keep track of how many you get back. This is a good indicator. If you get back 10%, you are doing great. Reality will probably be more like a 3 to 5% return. That is very good and you have the advantage of knowing immediately what is working and what is being ignored

7. Ad gimmicks. This includes coffee cups, pens, match books, key-chains and more. The list is almost endless. Most towns have an advertising agency that has access to everything you ever wanted to put your name on. Before you hire one of these agencies, check out the possibility of doing your own sub-contracting for these items. Most quick-print places offer quite a few of these items at lower rates and they usually have a monthly special. Local ceramic shops can do custom mugs and your neighborhood screen printer offers an endless variety of shirts, hats, mouse-pads etc. Use your imagination.

8. Radio and television. This is the expensive way to get people's attention and is usually reserved for high ticket items like cars, house siding or a business that can have a large stock rotation. This type of advertising can also be used to build up a recognition factor. If you have a product or service that falls into these categories and you can afford it, then you will want to consider this option. Quite often a nationally recognized product will offer co-op advertising. This is when they run an ad for their product and mention or write in your business at the end. The rates for this type of advertising are much lower than a full commercial rate and you should look hard at this if it is offered. (Example: RCA would run an ad and say "and these products can be purchased at YOUR STORE in YOUR TOWN.)

9. Consider internet advertising. Type into your search engine "free classified ads" and you will be surprised at how many sites there are where you can advertise at no cost.

10. Community Involvement. What? If you sponsor a baseball team, for example, your business name will be on every jersey that the players wear. Kids wear these jerseys out in public. Parents will see your name during every game and there are always other stops that are made traveling to and from the games. You can also partner with other groups like your local police department, schools and just about any other organization that could use your help. They don't usually mind if your name is on whatever service you are providing as long as you are helping out.

Opening Your Business

Have enough cash up front to cover at least six months total expenses. A year is better. Total expenses mean just that. It needs to cover everything including living expenses. Make sure that you have product available. Have all of the tools you need in place. Pre-advertise the date that you are going to open. If you are going into the retail side, make sure that you allow plenty of time on the date to renovate and to get your equipment and product in place. Make sure that everyone that you ever knew or think that you ever will know is aware that you are opening for business. Try and have any and all the media present that is possible for publicity. (Often your local Chamber of Commerce will have a ribbon cutting if you are a Chamber member.)

Take pictures that can be turned into press releases. Have a Grand Opening, if you can, and hold a drawing or give away prizes. Do anything you can to attract positive, tasteful attention. (Balloons - clowns - lights - an ape - you get the picture). Make everyone feel welcome and that they feel good about being there. Don't just talk to your friends. Make sure you speak to everyone that shows up.

Smile. Don't be nervous. Don't worry about sales today. Don't turn down business, but don't force it either.

Hiring and training your employees

There are several points to look at in this area. In your mind, you know what you want in the way of service for your customers. It will be up to you to hire and then train your employees to provide this service. You can be a nice person and still demand from them a certain level of efficiency and dependability.

Before hiring anyone

First, decide on what you want to or can pay. Pay is why people work. If the salary is going to depend on experience or education, decide on a scale. Have in mind how much raises will be and when they will be offered. If you know this in advance it will be harder to be taken advantage of.

Hiring

First, get in your mind exactly what you want in the way of an employee. This is probably where you figure out that the chances are your cousin will not be the right person for the job, even if you are getting pressure from your relatives to hire them because they have "special problems". Conduct interviews in order to select the person that you think will best fit into your idea of what you want. When you are conducting your interviews, outline everything that you expect from them. It will be best if it is in writing in case you face a need for documentation later. Explain to them that there is a 90-day probation period in order to make sure that they will work out and that during that period they can be dismissed for a wide variety of reasons that do not require explanation.
Keep in mind the fact that there are federal and state laws governing employment.

Training

After you select your employee, it is important that they receive proper training. Only you know what you want out of this person, so it will be up to you to make sure that the employee is up to speed on all services, equipment functions, any machinery that they will run and all safety aspects involved with the job. It is also up to you to make sure that they have the correct attitude when dealing with customers. This includes proper phone etiquette. You can best train by example and if you set a bad one, they may follow it.

Charities

Once your business is opened, you will be asked by many charitable organizations for donations. I am of the opinion that you owe it to your community to give back something to those that support you and your business. You will probably want to give to all of them but will quickly discover that if you gave a dollar to every one of them you would go broke. Decide on those that you wish to donate to very carefully. Things to keep in mind are:

1. Which ones do the most good for the community? It will not hurt you to personally investigate which of those groups asking for money actually do something for the community. Ask about the percentage of monies given back to the local area as opposed to salaries. If a group is bringing in $100,000.00, paying out $90,000.00 in salaries and giving back $10,000.00 to your town then perhaps you will want to think twice before funding them. Maybe you have a pet project that could use your help. In our community we had a woman that fed about thirty needy children, in her neighborhood, breakfast every school day. Although she was only earning a poverty level income, she still did this in her home and out of her own pocket with no help from anyone. Imagine her surprise when she was offered a little financial help out of the blue. This woman did more for her community than many agencies. All that I am saying is help those who help the most.

2. Which ones give you the highest visibility? A sign in the office of your favorite charity stating that such and such was furnished by your company is not a bad thing. Neither is your company logo on equipment or supplies that are on display hurtful to your cause. Are they willing to give you a plug at their fund-raisers or dinners? All of this ads to your credibility.

3. Which ones might accept service instead of monetary donations? You might find that there is often a greater need for

your service or product in an organization than there is for money. Keep in mind that these products or services are just as deductible (and often at retail full value) as cash when tax time comes.

4. Which ones might funnel you business later on? Quite often the members of a group that you have supported might have a need of your product or services outside of the group. If your product or service is above average then it would only stand to reason that they would come to you since you have supported them in their need. They should also recommend you to their family and friends and introduce you into the companies that they work for. Ask for their help in securing more business. Just make sure that your product or service is beyond reproach.

This all may sound crass to you but it is only good business. We would all like to give from the bottom of our hearts and ask for no recognition and if you want to do it that way, then go ahead. We often "snuck" a little cash to some of our pet small agencies and never told them who we were, but we also availed ourselves of the advantages of high profile gifts that would bring us more business.

Warning: There are many false agencies out there that sound good but that are merely fronts for scams. I gave freely to several different police agencies. It is my personal belief that these agencies do a lot of good in our community, particularly with youngsters. Somehow we got on a list and were besieged by a large number of "police charities" that were false. Many of them had names so close to the ones that we gave to that it was hard to tell the difference. It took us a while to weed through the bad ones and report them to the real police. Just be aware of what is out there and don't be afraid to insist on something in writing. If they refuse then you can assume that they are not legit. Call the Better Business Bureau and check up on them before you give anyone anything unless you know them personally and trust them.

101 Low Cost Business Ideas to Use or Modify

Under $ 1,000.00 Start-up

1. Consulting in your area of expertise
2. Training in your area of expertise
3. Digital Photography
4. Fishing/Canoeing/Outdoor Guide
5. Handyman/Odd job/Fix-it service
6. Custom Cake/Pastry Baking
7. Develop Hobby Kits (Beer Making Kits, Birdhouse Kits, etc.)
8. In-town package/parcel delivery service
9. Perpetual garage sale
10. Personal errand running/Shopping
11. Home/Office cleaning service
12. Window washing
13. Word processing service
14. Gift Baskets (food, cosmetics, potpourri, etc)
15. Interior/exterior painting service
16. Balloon delivery service
17. Telemarketing service
18. Computer tutor
19. Web page design
20. Resume service
21. Free community newsletter/things-to-do-around-town information sheet supported by local advertisers
22. Genealogy research
23. Disc jockey/ Karyoke
24. Wedding planner
25. Party planner
26. Party entertainment (clown, magician, etc)
27. Home inventory business
28. Car detailing service
29. Plant service
30. Power tool rental service

31. Install security systems
32. Personal trainer
33. Personal chef/dietician
34. Pool cleaning service
35. Rain gutter/spout cleaning service
36. House checking/pet feeding/mail & paper pick-up service
37. Dog walking service
38. Senior citizen sitting service
39. Garage/storeroom cleaning service
40. Interior design/redesign
41. Form a "temp" agency

E- Business Under $ 1,000.00 Start-up

42. E-commerce – Web site
43. Start Internet classified placement service
44. Sell items on Internet Auctions (This can be tied to any product.)
45. Co-op web mall with many different products. You sell your product and also get percentage from other mall members on your site.

Under $ 2,000.00 Start-up

46. Lawn care/Landscaping service
47. Trash removal service
48. Chimney Sweep
49. Vending Route (candy machines, etc)
50. Power cleaning (fences, decks, driveways, etc)
51. Holiday decorating service
52. Parking lot cleaning and striping
53. Mail-order/drop shipping (be careful who you do business with)
54. Carpet cleaning

If you own a truck and/or trailer

55. Light hauling or moving
56. Store delivery and set-up
57. Firewood delivery
58. Selling your/any product on the road at fairs and festivals

Using Your Home

59. Bed & Breakfast
60. Limited babysitting
61. Limited pet sitting
62. Craft lessons in your studio
63. Art studio selling your art or others creations in private showings
64. Custom sewing and monogramming
65. Furniture refinishing
66. Designer Clothing of your own design

Flea Market booth Ideas

67. Christmas Shop
68. Specialty craft supplies
69. Used books, either general or specialty
70. Vintage clothing sales
71. Used furniture sales
72. Art of different types
73. Children's toys, games and clothing
74. Collectibles
75. Kitchen specialties

Ideas Requiring Land or Retail Space

76. Lawn ornaments/Mexican Imports

77. Pet Cemetery
78. Pet retirement center
79. Pet Hotel
80. Growing herbs
81. Growing organic foods
82. Starting artist's co-op
83. Used car "lemon lot" People park their used car on your lot and you get a percentage when it sells. You can also slip in some of your own vehicles.

Writing/Creative Projects

84. Specialty cookbook
85. Consulting Materials
86. How-To Books or Videos
87. Novels
88. Greeting Cards
89. Poetry Contests
90. Children's Games
91. Wedding/Special event/Pet still photography
92. Wedding/Special event video taping service
93. Children's books
94. Be an artist/sculptor

Craft Ideas

95. Create Christmas Line of Ornaments, Plates, etc.
96. Create Custom Design Iron On decals
97. Wood Projects (bird houses, toys, etc)
98. Custom design furniture
99. Create seasonal vests and shirts
100. Create your own line of potpourri

Business Check-List

- ❑ Have you and are you keeping all of your receipts?

- ❑ Have you decided on exactly what service or product you want to introduce?

- ❑ Have you made sure that there is a need or market?

- ❑ Have you designed and developed your product?

- ❑ Have you determined a real cost on your product?

- ❑ Do you know what you want to market inside and out?

- ❑ Have you formed a marketing plan?

- ❑ Have you compiled a list of business prospects and contacts?

- ❑ Have you checked free local resources like colleges, SCORE, small business development centers and others to see what help is available to you?

- ❑ Have you learned all you can about the competition?

- ❑ Have you developed your company's image the way you want it?

- ❑ Have you selected the work place/space where you will conduct business and seen that it is properly prepared for the business that you want to conduct?

- ❑ Have you established a line of credit and a list of business references?

- Have you set up an accounting process that will allow you to keep an accurate track of your costs and, in the future, your profits?

- Have you protected your product or business through copyrights/patents/laws and protected your product and yourself from liability with insurance, incorporation and/or other tools?

- Is your advertising in place and ready to go?

- Do you have enough cash to see yourself through 6 months total expenses?

- Are all of your employees properly trained and familiar with your product and equipment?

About the Author

What makes us qualified to tell you what we think you need to do in order to start a successful business? I guess that the answer would have to be experience. The following is a list of retail operations that my wife, son and I have owned. Not all three of us were involved with every business but my wife and I worked in every one except for the first, which I worked alone. This list does not include a few out-of-the-house enterprises such as author, art gallery, furniture refinishing service, perpetual garage sale, moving service or some of the side-lines I had when I was in the Navy. Our team has roughly 88 years of combined business experience to draw from and pass along to you.

1. Pennbrook Lawn Service (My first business was started when I was 14 and continued through High School. This developed into a full time business and I probably had more expendable income then than at any other time in my life.)

2. The Highway 67 Antique Shop and Flea Market (Our first venture into retail in adult life. Many lessons were learned here, most of which were bitter. This was the only business that we owned that we lost money in.)

3. Highway 67 Discount Furniture (An adjunct to the Antique Store that just naturally developed. In itself, it was profitable.)

4.Robertson Photography (We functioned as a freelance team working for companies such as 3M, Pepsi, The Davis Cup Finals for UPI, a movie premier, etc.)

5. Video Express (The third video tape store in the state of Arkansas. It was a great business started at a great time and it allowed us to move up to a much nicer life style. Our son started working in this business at the age of 12 when we added a line of computers. By the age of 14 he had a regular group of college students that he did consulting work for.)

6. Encore Video (Another video tape store in a town 10 miles down the road. Our son managed it when he turned 16 and could get there on his own.)

7. Video Express Productions (A full 3-camera VHS production studio and editing suite that was added as a separate entity to Video Express and sold as a separate business.)

8. Rupert's On The Rocks (A bar/restaurant that started in an environment that was somewhat less than ideal. Bullet holes were patched, the building painted and the motif was changed to a sports bar theme with live music on the weekends. Clientele changed and so did the ambience. It ended up being a good and safe place to enjoy an evening. Profit realized and fantasy satisfied.)

9. Robertson Technologies (At it's inception, Robertson Technologies was designed to supply large companies as well as individuals with Hi-tech products such as custom built computer systems, computer parts, software, networking and other related items. Due to the demand for our services we moved our headquarters to the TCBY Building's lobby after only one year in business. The TCBY Building is the tallest building and the most prestigious address in Arkansas. The company was sold in 1999.)

10. Robertson Arms Company (No, it wasn't a hotel. We bought and restored antique guns, swords and other weapons. We sold the company when we moved our residence to Fairfield Bay.)

11. Support Services (The title just about covers it all. We do not advertise this business because we are so well known in the local industry. I am still asked to freelance in various capacities, provide talent or I am retained as a consultant, so the business lives on.)

12. Robertson Consulting (This business was formed as a result of various people coming to us and asking for our help in starting their new business. So far it has been the most enjoyable.)

13. PubHubBooks (An on-line bookstore that we've had for seven years now. It keeps us busy and our minds sharp.)

www.ingramcontent.com/pod-product-compliance
Lightning Source LLC
Chambersburg PA
CBHW071008180526
45168CB00003B/1340